P9-CBE-267

⚙ The ⚙
BLACKSMITHS

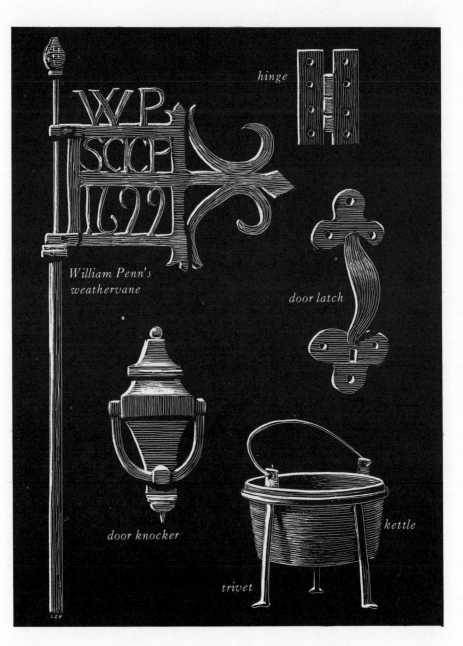

hinge

WP
SCCF
1699

William Penn's
weathervane

door latch

door knocker

trivet

kettle

COLONIAL AMERICAN CRAFTSMEN

The

BLACKSMITHS

WRITTEN & ILLUSTRATED BY

Leonard Everett Fisher

FRANKLIN WATTS, INC.
New York, London, 1976

Library of Congress Cataloging in Publication Data

Fisher, Leonard Everett.
    The blacksmiths.

    (Colonial American craftsmen)
    SUMMARY: Introduces the history of black-
smithing and discusses the techniques, products, well-
known blacksmiths, and commercial importance of
this trade in colonial America.
    1. Blacksmithing — United States — History —
Juvenile literature. 2. Blacksmiths — United States —
Juvenile literature. 3. United States — History —
Colonial period. ca. 1600–1775 — Juvenile literature.
[1. Blacksmithing—History. 2. Blacksmiths. 3. United
States — History — Colonial period, ca. 1600–1775]
I. Title.
TT220.F57   338.4'7'682   75–26684
ISBN 0–531–02901–8

Colonial Americans

===

THE ARCHITECTS
THE BLACKSMITHS
THE CABINETMAKERS
THE DOCTORS
THE GLASSMAKERS
THE HATTERS
THE HOMEMAKERS
THE PAPERMAKERS
THE PEDDLERS
THE POTTERS
THE PRINTERS
THE SCHOOLMASTERS
THE SHIPBUILDERS
THE SHOEMAKERS
THE SILVERSMITHS
THE TANNERS
THE WEAVERS
THE WIGMAKERS

===

A Short History

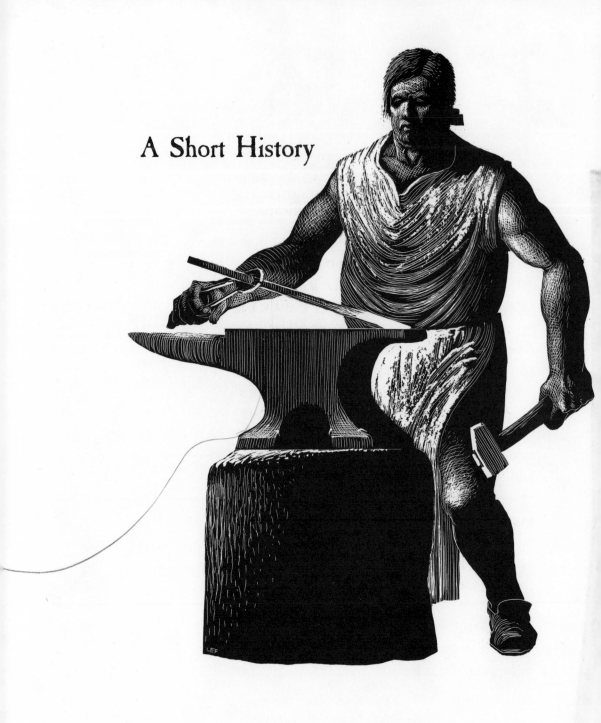

To most people, the old-time blacksmith was a burly man who spent his working day shoeing horses. To the colonists of early America, the blacksmith was a jack-of-all-iron-trades. He was as important to colonial endurance as he was to the well-being of a horse. In the beginning of colonization there were more blacksmiths in British America than there were horses. The colonial American craftsman who did nothing but shoe horses was called a *farrier*.

This jack-of-all-iron-trades — the colonial American blacksmith — spent his long working day hammering, or *forging*, red-hot iron into an assortment of tools used to clear the rough land and build a civilization: axes and adzes, hoes, sickles and scythes, plow blades, barrel hoops, kettles and pots. He made latches, hinges, locks and nails, weathervanes, andirons, gates, fences, grilles, and wheel parts. And he repaired everything made of iron. Once in a while one became a gunsmith forging gun barrels, cannons, and other useful weapons.

If the colonial blacksmith operated his forge in or near the shipyards that dotted the eastern shoreline of America, he was at the center of America's most important industry — shipbuilding. Here he made ship fittings and hardware of every description: anchors and anchor chains; rudder irons; shipwright tools; hooks, rings, and bolts.

In 1585 English colonists at Roanoke Island, Virginia, discovered iron *ore* in nearby marshes. They called the soft surface ore *bog iron*. Unfortunately, these would-be settlers did not stay long enough in the New World to do anything about it. Beaten by the wilderness, they returned to England the following year.

Twenty-one years later, in the spring of 1607, another band of Englishmen tried to establish themselves in Virginia. This time they stayed. Their tiny settlement-fort, Jamestown, became the first permanent British colony in North America. Among the 104 or 105 settlers were a few essential craftsmen, including James Read, a blacksmith.

Despite disease, starvation, death, marauding Indians, treachery, and a general inability to cope with the hostile environment, the Jamestown settlers somehow clung to their fragile toehold in Virginia. Eventually, braced by some

The *HISTORY*

laboring newcomers, they managed to ship back to their sponsors, the Virginia Company, samples, or "tryals," of pitch, tar, glass, timber, and bog iron.

But the Jamestown settlers still depended on the cargoes of food, goods, and supplies brought to the colony in English ships. The colonists needed more than the blacksmith could provide in the way of iron products. In the early autumn of 1620, the ship *Supply* arrived in Virginia. Among the hundreds of items she carried were 22,500 nails, 2,000 hobnails, 100 iron hoops, 66 axes and hatchets, 70 hoes and spades, 14 scythes, 4 chisels, 2 gouges, 4 handsaws, 25 augers, 1 anvil, and a "vise for a smyth." Each of these things was necessary if the settlers were to endure in the raw Virginia wilderness.

The Jamestown colony weathered its first miserable years, including a devastating massacre and a plague that reduced a population of twelve hundred men, women, and children to three hundred. By 1625 the colony had expanded beyond the original one-acre fort. There were now twenty-seven separate communities along the James River. The colonists had produced glass bottles, constructed a ship, and made barrels. They had also built a simple furnace to sep-

foot-operated bellows

arate iron from its boggy ore. With this furnace the colonists were able to produce a few *blooms*, or globs, of iron, which were slammed into bars called *bar iron*. The blacksmith then hammered the bar iron into useful products. Yet the wilderness first had to yield to the ax if the colonists were to have any hope of establishing themselves in North America with safety and permanence.

Most of the first axes used in America to cut down trees to build forts and houses were *felling axes*. While most of these were wrought in England, a few, perhaps, were forged by Jamestown blacksmiths. Between the 1620s and the 1640s very little bar iron came out of settlement furnaces. The process of refining iron ore — chiefly bog iron — was too difficult to handle in the largely uncivilized colony.

It was not until the late 1640s that a workable blast furnace was built in present-day Saugus, Massachusetts, assuring the ten thousand colonists of that area an ample supply of iron, *pig iron*. The blast furnace separated the metal from the ore. As the molten metal ran out of the furnace through a channel, it was collected in a series of sand molds called *pigs* — hence the name, pig iron. The Saugus ironworks produced

not only bar and pig iron but *rolled* and sheet, or *plate*, iron as well.

The first axes used by colonial Americans had an additional use besides knocking down trees. Neighboring Indians had no iron or iron implements. They had no axes. The colonists seized the opportunity to barter their axes for whatever the Indians had that was needed at the moment — food, pelts, information, even peace. The Indians were pleased to have the axes, if not altogether grateful.

Those bartered axes were known as *trade axes*. Soon American blacksmiths produced a short-handled, hatchetlike ax — a half-size felling ax — to be used as a trade ax. It looked like a tomahawk. And that is exactly what it turned out to be — a tomahawk. Many a settler's last look at life was the mean end of a trade ax made by a local blacksmith that the settler had himself traded away.

From the time the Saugus ironworks was established until 1750 — a period of about one hundred years — England paid little attention to American blacksmiths. During this period the number of blacksmiths in the colonies had increased so rapidly that they began to outnumber ship-

wrights, wigmakers, joiners, silversmiths, and most other craftsmen in America.

Not all these blacksmiths were English, or white, for that matter. Most of the blacksmiths who worked in Pennsylvania were of German descent. New Jersey had a large contingent of German and Swedish blacksmiths. Those who worked on the huge southern plantations were black slaves. While nearly every colony had its full share of furnaces, forges, and larger ironworks by 1750, most of the ironmaking activity was concentrated in the lower New England and Middle Atlantic colonies. Pennsylvania, however, became the center of colonial American ironmaking.

For a long time, England had imported most of its iron from Sweden. Swedish iron, the best in the world, hammered into materials by British blacksmiths, found ready markets in the burgeoning American colonies. But as American iron production and know-how improved, the colonies became less and less dependent on British iron imports. Britain's American iron market began to dry up. At the same time, Sweden began to raise the prices of its iron exports to Britain. By 1750 the British iron industry, caught between Swedish prices and American self-reliance, teetered on the edge of ruin.

In 1750 Parliament passed the Iron Act "to encourage the Importation of Pig and Bar Iron from His Majesty's Colonies in *America*; and to prevent the Erection of any Mill or other Engine for Slitting or Rolling of Iron; or any Plateing Forge to work with a Tilt Hammer; or any Furnace for making Steel in any of the said Colonies."

The whole idea of the Act was to balance Britain's iron economy rather than to destroy colonial American iron enterprise. Britain hoped to keep its forges and furnaces supplied with good-quality but inexpensive colonial bar and pig iron and eliminate expensive Swedish iron as a major source. The Act would put British blacksmiths and ironworkers back on the job, while holding back American production of cannons, cannonballs, iron shot, and more.

Although the Iron Act encouraged British users to purchase American bar and pig iron by reducing restrictive duties levied on these goods at British ports of entry, it never really succeeded. While British demand for American iron soared, Britain could not prevent the colonial ironworker from forging anything he pleased. There was just too much iron in America to regulate and too many first-rate colonial blacksmiths.

Finally, the Revolution exploded in Massachusetts on April 19, 1775. In the difficult struggle that followed, few blacksmiths served as fighting men. Instead, they were kept busy forging and repairing the iron tools of war.

One typically busy blacksmith, Peter Townsend, was hired by the Continental Congress in 1778 to forge a huge, indestructible iron chain. The Congress wanted to stretch such a chain across a narrow neck of New York's Hudson River in the vicinity of West Point to prevent the northward passage of British naval vessels. Townsend, with the help of an army of workmen, labored a month and a half and produced the chain. It was at least five hundred yards long. Each link measured approximately one by three feet. The chain was hauled in sections to West Point and floated on logs across the river. It was held fast by iron anchors, which Townsend and his crew also made. It remained intact until it was dismantled at the end of the Revolutionary War. The British never breached the chain.

It seems, almost, that from the very beginning of colonization the American blacksmith, with his hammer, anvil, and fiery forge, was as much a symbol of colonial will and determination as was the unyielding hardness of the iron he used.

How the Blacksmiths Worked

THERE WERE NO SCHOOLS OR BOOKS to teach someone to be a blacksmith during the colonial period. The varying methods and ancient skills were passed from one generation to the next, from father to son, from master to apprentice, from the Old World to the New World.

Tools and techniques were similar from shop to shop, to be sure. But no two collections of tools or their uses were exactly alike. Not even the interior arrangements of the blacksmiths' working areas were alike — similar, perhaps, but not identical. Every blacksmith had his own way with iron to suit himself and the work he did.

A smith anywhere in rural Connecticut who made candlestands and shod horses in his spare time had a different approach to working the iron than, for example, a Pennsylvania blacksmith who specialized in making hinges and plow blades. And these two craftsmen differed again from the seaside smith of New Hampshire who made anchors and chains, or the South Carolina blacksmith slave who forged every conceivable item necessary to the functioning of the plantation. There was also the isolated farmer who

made and repaired whatever iron items he needed to work his land and keep his house in good condition.

Basically, the work of the blacksmith was to shape or repair a piece of iron having some useful or decorative purpose. To do this, he had to heat the iron to make it *malleable* — that is, soft and workable. And to do this, every smith had to have a special fireplace called a *hearth.*

The *TECHNIQUE*

The hearth — a rectangular brick structure — jutted out from one side of a stone chimney into the shop. The hearth contained a waist-high well, about a foot deep, that held a charcoal fire. Usually there was a counter at the far end of the hearth where the smith could lay down a tool or let an iron piece cool. Behind the chimney and connected to the fire well by a tunnel was a *bellows.* The bellows was used to pump air into the fire to bring it alive and to a great heat. Sometimes the blacksmith operated the bellows himself by yanking a handy pole-and-chain contraption connected to it. Often as not, the bellows was operated by an apprentice who began his seven years of training learning to regulate the fire under the watchful eye of the master blacksmith.

Apprentices and journeymen assistants were a

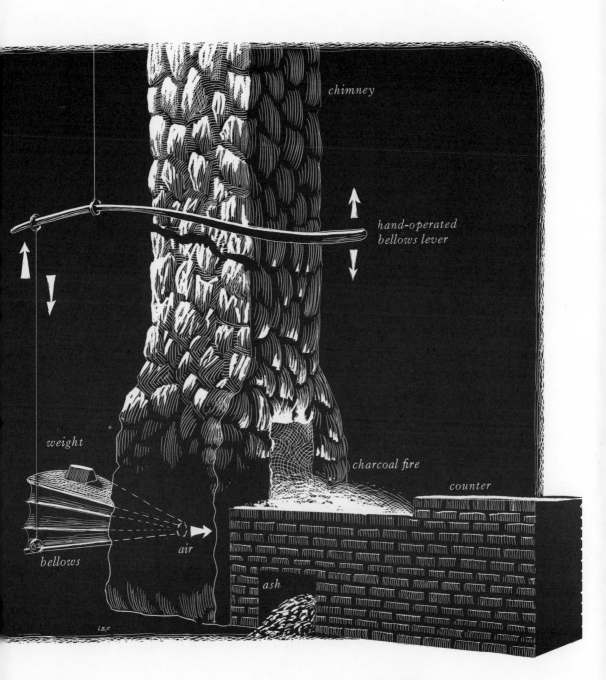

chimney

hand-operated
bellows lever

weight

charcoal fire

counter

bellows

air

ash

❁ 25 ❁

The *TECHNIQUE*

common sight around the colonial blacksmith shop. Often the work of the blacksmith could not be done by one man working alone. If the iron pieces he was forging were small, that was one thing. They were easy to handle. But if the iron pieces were large, he needed help. Iron was heavy, hard to move around, and difficult for one man to maneuver. The blacksmith might have a tough time trying to grip a large, white-hot bar with his *tongs*, bang it into shape with a heavy hammer, and operate the bellows all at the same time. There were many opportunities for beginners in the colonial blacksmith shop.

If there was any single method followed by every smith, regardless of his skills and specialties, it was the use of *charcoal* to fuel his fire. The charcoal used by the colonial blacksmith was chiefly pure *carbon*. Carbon is a basic nonmetallic element found in organic substances. The colonial blacksmith's charcoal was produced by slowly burning, without the help of air, a conelike pile of hard woods. If the air supply to the cone was either limited or cut off, the burning wood was not likely to be consumed by flames and turned into a mound of ashes. Instead, the smoldering wood was charred through and through. The com-

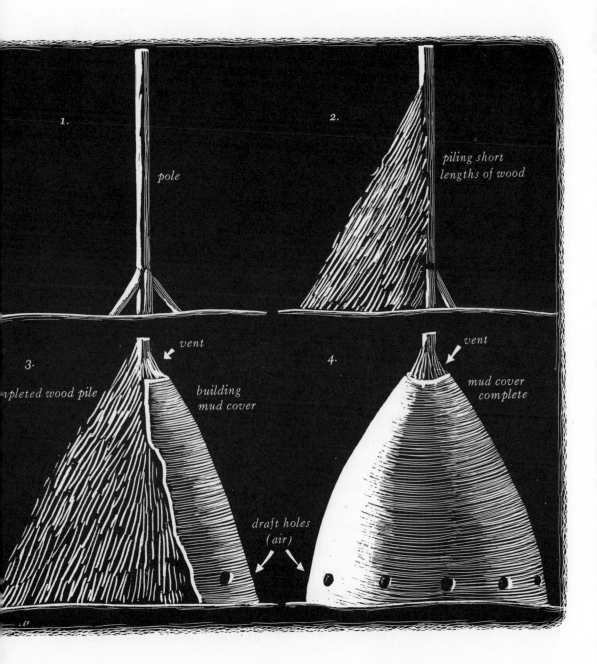

1.

pole

2.

piling short
lengths of wood

3.

...pleted wood pile

vent

building
mud cover

4.

vent

mud cover
complete

draft holes
(air)

pletely charred or "carbonized" wood became charcoal when cool.

Charcoal fire fuel was important for several reasons. It was easily made from the vast amount of hard woods that grew in the colonial wilderness. It was readily obtainable and very cheap. Burning charcoal was smokeless, a distinct advantage to the blacksmith who worked indoors at an open hearth. Last, and most important, was the fact that carbon, or in the case of the blacksmith, charcoal, burned at hotter temperatures than plain uncarbonized wood.

Charcoal was also used as a fire fuel for *smelting*, or refining iron — the heating process by which nearly pure iron is extracted from the ore. As the iron ore was heated and impurities were drawn off in the form of waste, the iron particles began to fuse and absorb carbon from the burning charcoal. The near-molten, spongy mass of hot iron, or bloom, was heated in a different furnace, pounded, and reheated to reduce the amount of carbon in it. This low-carbon-content iron was then slammed into a bar. (The early forge at Saugus had a large water-powered hammer to do the job.) The resulting bar was called *wrought iron*. It was much sought after because

The *TECHNIQUE*

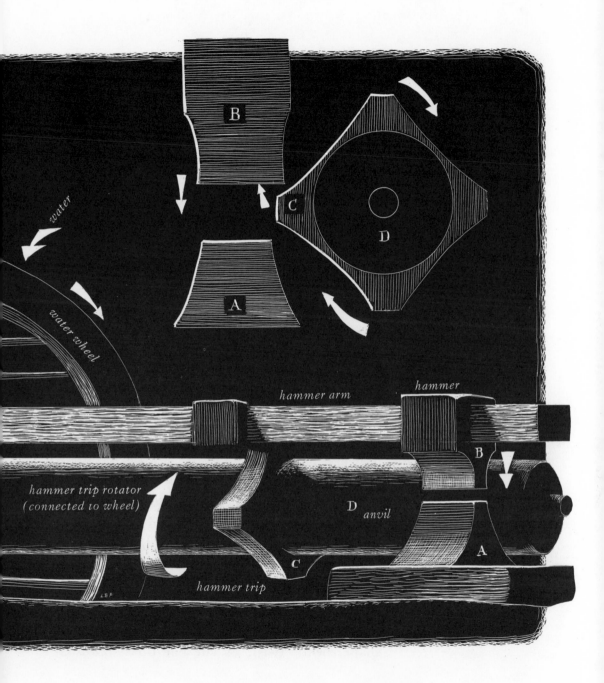

water

water wheel

B

C

D

A

hammer arm

hammer

hammer trip rotator
(connected to wheel)

B

D *anvil*

A

C

hammer trip

it was very workable yet extremely tough. And it did not rust.

The charcoal fire was central to everything the smith made. Without a perfect fire to soften the iron he could not lengthen or widen it, a process called *drawing*. Nor could he thicken and shorten, or *upset*, the iron; *weld*, or join, two pieces; *punch*, or put a hole through it; or otherwise bend, twist, and cut it.

Too much reheating of the iron accompanied by swift cooling dips in a bucket of water would make the iron brittle. Even a high-grade wrought iron could become brittle in this way. If the iron became too brittle, the blacksmith *annealed* it. He brought it to a red-hot state and allowed it to cool slowly by itself, to make it more resilient once again. The smith had to know the nature of his iron and how to use the fire for best results.

No blacksmith could hope to do much of anything without an *anvil*. The anvil was a heavy iron block on which he hammered his pieces into shape. One end of the anvil — the *heel* — was blunt. A sharp *horn* projected from the other end. A couple of holes pierced the heel. These holes held a variety of interchangeable devices used to shape, bend, twist, or cut hot iron — *hardies,*

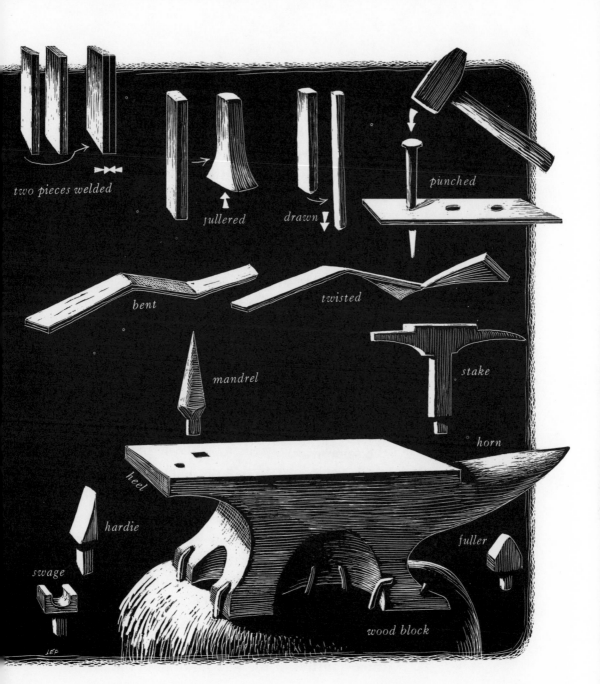

two pieces welded

fullered

drawn

punched

bent

twisted

mandrel

stake

horn

heel

hardie

swage

wood block

fuller

swages, fullers, mandrels, stakes, and more. The anvil was fixed to a heavy wood post that was sunk deep in the ground to make it rigid, solid, and nonvibrating.

The *TECHNIQUE*

Of all the countless iron objects made by the colonial blacksmith, the ordinary nail was, perhaps, the simplest to produce. Nails for house-building were in great demand. And just about every blacksmith made nails.

There were many different types of nails (spikes and tacks too). There were nails for flooring, trim and fancy moldings, window and picture frames, house rafters, barn studs, roofing, and any wood pieces that had to be held together. Generally they were all made by hand and in about the same way.

First the smith heated the end of a *nailrod* — a two- or three-foot-long rectangular strip of iron. When the end became red-hot, he placed it on the anvil and rapidly hammered the glowing tip into a four-sided point. Next he placed the four-sided pointed strip on a *hardie* — a wrought-iron blade whose square-pegged bottom fit into one of the holes in the heel of the anvil. With one smart blow of his hammer, the smith drove the strip about three-quarters of the way down onto the hardie,

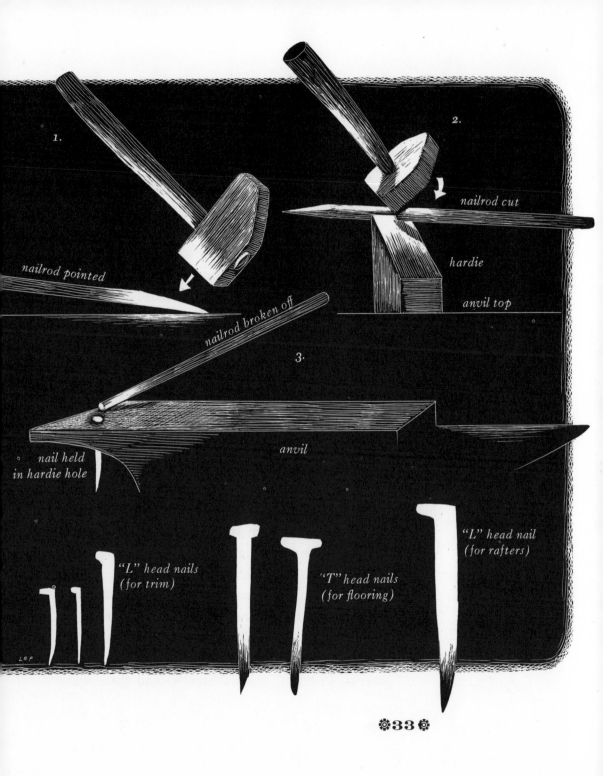

1.

nailrod pointed

2.

nailrod cut

hardie

anvil top

nailrod broken off

3.

nail held
in hardie hole

anvil

"L" head nails
(for trim)

"T" head nails
(for flooring)

"L" head nail
(for rafters)

LEP

❖33❖

The *TECHNIQUE*

partially cutting it at a desired length. The nearly cut and pointed rod, still glowing hot, was thrust through another square hole in the heel of the anvil and broken off. The top of the protruding nail was beaten and flattened. The nail quickly cooled, shrank, and was easily knocked out of the hole. Some blacksmiths used a device called a *nailheader* — a heavy iron bar with a hole at one or both ends. It could be held in a vise or made rigid in some other way. Whatever method he used, the smith used the nailheader as he did the hole in the anvil. The results were similar.

The ax was a fairly simple tool to forge. The *head,* or iron part, of the ax was usually made in one of two ways. The blacksmith welded two separate pieces of red-hot iron and then forced the permanently joined pieces over an iron horn called a mandrel to make the *eye* that held the wood handle, or *helve.* He could also fold one red-hot piece of metal around an iron bar to form the eye.

The cutting edge of the ax was, very often, made of *steel.* Colonial steel, like present-day steel, was very hard iron. It was made hard by leaving the carbon absorbed during the smelting process. In effect, colonial steel — and there was

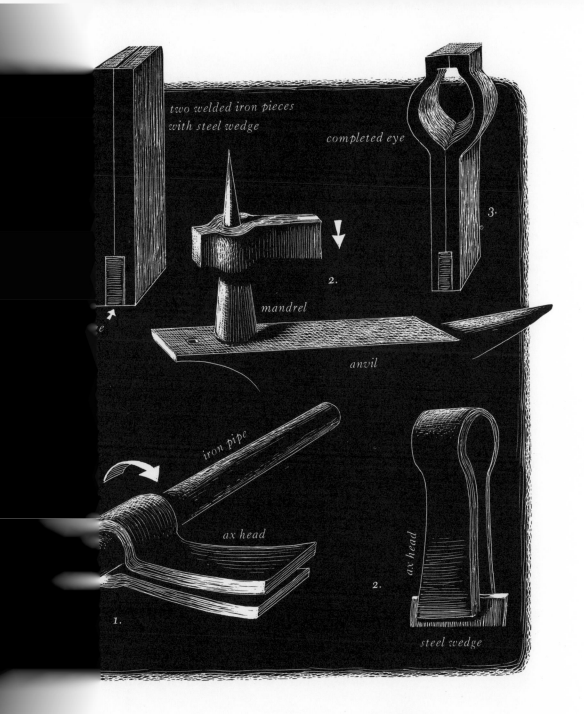

two welded iron pieces
with steel wedge

completed eye

3.

2.

mandrel

anvil

iron pipe

ax head

ax head

2.

1.

steel wedge

not that much of it — was handmade high-carbon-content iron.

Before the smith welded either his separate pieces or the folded bar, he inserted a steel wedge at what would be the cutting end of the ax head. All of this was heated, reheated, pounded, and repounded until the pieces were fused and the proper shape of the head achieved. The steel edge was reheated, hammered thin, and filed. The head was then annealed. Finally the cold steel cutting edge was filed to razor-sharpness and a handle was fitted through the eye.

For the first 125 years of colonization, the shape of the colonial ax was chiefly European. The helve was straight. The top of the head and the head itself formed a right angle to the helve. The cutting edge was arc-shaped. There was no *poll*, or hammer end. By 1750 colonial blacksmiths had developed a slightly different shape of ax. The newer shape had the same straight wood helve and the head set at a right angle to it. However, the cutting edge was now straight rather than arced. The blade had a top and bottom flare to it. And there was now a heavy poll at the back end of the head.

Although shoeing a horse was a minor part of

head

head

flat poll

eye

eye

helve

head

head

helve

LEF

❈ 37 ❈

the work of the colonial American blacksmith, it still required the skill of analyzing the proper shoe needed; handling the animal; *paring*, or cutting, and molding the hooves for a good fit; making the shoe itself and the right kind of nails to attach it; and finally fitting, nailing, and filing without hurting or abusing the horse in any way. And without being abused by the horse in return.

The *TECHNIQUE*

The first mechanical task to be done by the smith was to remove the old shoes. This he did by cradling each foot in his lap and carefully pulling out the eight nails used to attach the iron shoe. He had to be careful, because the last thing he wanted to do was to damage the wall of the hoof, making it more difficult to attach the new shoe. Next he pared down each hoof with a knife, cutting away the unwanted growth, giving the hoof a proper slope and a good flat, clean surface ready to receive the new shoe.

When both the blacksmith and the horse were satisfied with the feel and comfort of the pared hooves, the blacksmith went to his forge to make the shoes. The hot iron was heated and bent into shape around the horn of the anvil. The ends were bent up and a clip was welded to the front topside of the shoe. The clip kept the horse's hoof from

slipping on the shoe and gave it a snug fit. The blacksmith then matched the roughly finished shoe against the hoof for size. After some additional heating and hammering to flatten and smooth down the shoe, the smith punched eight rectangular nail holes in each shoe. The shoes were then nailed to the hooves in such a way that the nails went in at an angle and came out through the side of the hoof. The horse felt none of this, nor the paring either. Since the hoof has no nerves, the horse feels no pain there. In any case, the blacksmith pinched off the sharp ends of the nails and bent the blunt ends down. After a final and gentle filing to make the meeting of hoof and shoe even, the job was completed.

Most colonial blacksmiths fitted the shoes by shaping the iron rather than by overparing the hoof. A horse's hoof is not a solid mass. It is a wall that surrounds and protects the cushion and toe of the horse's foot. While the hoof itself is not sensitive, the cushion is. If the cushion was not protected properly by the hoof, severe damage would be the result. The horse might not be able to walk or trot or gallop correctly, if at all. And a lame horse was about as useless in colonial America as a musket without a trigger.

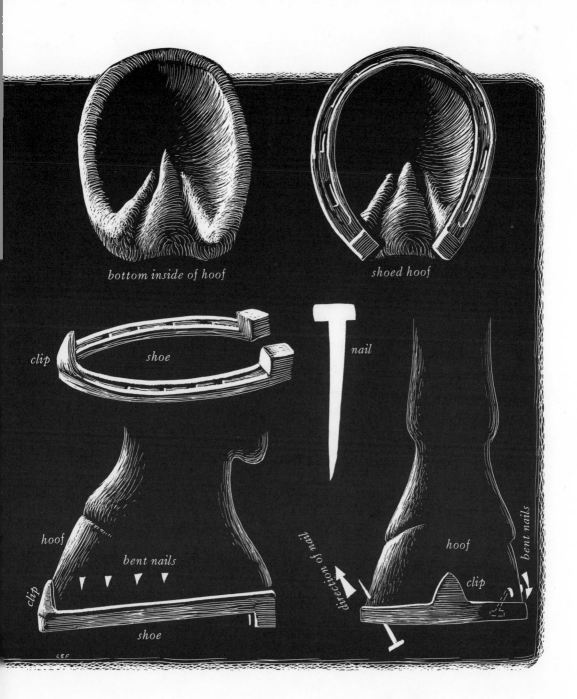

bottom inside of hoof

shoed hoof

clip

shoe

nail

hoof

bent nails

clip

shoe

direction of nail

hoof

clip

bent nails

LEF

The TECHNIQUE

Yet there were some blacksmiths who fitted the shoe by applying it red-hot against the hoof instead of working a bit more with the iron and paring more carefully. While the horse did not necessarily feel the searing heat, and while the heat of the pressing iron shoe made the hoof conform exactly to the shape of the shoe, too much of the hoof disappeared in the process. It would take some months before the hoof grew out, and in the meantime the horse might not be able to function too well.

The blacksmith in the colonies went on to other work after shoeing a horse. He might have been making an iron fence before the horse was brought to his shop. And in all probability he continued the fence not long after the horse was led away. Or perhaps he was just finishing a pair of heavy hinges for the jailhouse door. Like all the other craftsmen who worked in colonial America, the blacksmith's day was long and difficult. There was a lot to be done in the fast-growing country.

The colonial blacksmith with that tremendous supply of iron ore beneath his tired feet would be the key to America's destiny. America would one day lead the world in the production of iron and steel, becoming a world leader in technological and industrial development.

Blacksmiths' Terms

ANNEALING — The reheating and slow cooling of metal to eliminate its brittleness and strengthen it.

ANVIL — A heavy iron block on which metal is hammered and shaped.

BAR IRON — A rectangular block of refined iron.

BELLOWS — An accordionlike device for pumping air into a fire.

BLAST FURNACE — A furnace in which a blast of air creates the intense heat necessary to separate iron from its impurities.

BLOOM — A near-molten, spongy glob of iron ready to be hammered into a bar.

BOG IRON — Iron ore found in marshes.

CAST IRON — Iron made in a mold. Its carbon content is less than that of steel and more than that of wrought iron. It is softer than steel but harder than wrought iron.

DRAWING — To stretch or flatten the iron and reduce its bulk or thickness.

FARRIER — A blacksmith who shoes horses.

FORGE — To shape hot metal. A furnace for heating metal. A place where metal is hammered into objects.

FULLER — A tool for pounding grooves into iron.

HARDIE — A chisellike tool that fits vertically into the heel of the anvil.

HARDIE HOLE — The square hole in the heel of the anvil into which the hardie fits.

HEEL — The blunt end of the anvil.

HORN — The sharply pointed end of the anvil.

MALLEABLE — Metal that can be hammered, twisted, or reshaped without breaking.

MANDREL — A round, hornlike tool for shaping iron.

NAILHEADER — A tool used for flattening the top of a nail.

NAILROD — A slender iron rod used for nailmaking.

ORE — A mass of minerals and other substances taken from the earth, from which a metal is extracted.

PIG IRON — Near-molten iron collected from the furnace in a series of sand molds called *pigs*.

PLATE IRON — A thin, flat iron sheet.

ROLLED IRON — A cylindrical bar of iron.

SMELTING — The process of refining, or removing the impurities from iron ore and extracting the metal.

STAKE — A small anvil that fits into the hardie hole of a larger anvil.

STEEL — Very hard, high-carbon-content iron.

SWAGE — Any one of a variety of partially hollowed-out or half-round tools for shaping iron.

UPSETTING — To thicken and shorten a piece of iron.

WELDING — To join permanently two or more pieces of iron by heat.

WROUGHT IRON — A tough but bendable, workable piece of iron having little carbon.

Index

Since graduating from the Yale University School of Fine Arts (B.F.A. 1949; M.F.A. 1950), Leonard Everett Fisher has pursued a diverse career: painter; illustrator of some two hundred children's books — author of thirty of these; designer of United States postage stamps, posters, wall decorations, commemorative medals, and other works. A World War II army mapmaker and Winchester Fellow of Yale, he has been the recipient of a Pulitzer painting prize, a Connecticut League of Historical Societies citation, a Connecticut State Arts Commission grant, citations from the American Institute of Graphic Arts, and an international graphics award. He is represented in such collections as the Library of Congress, the Butler Institute of American Art, the New Britain Museum of American Art, and Mount Holyoke College. The University of Oregon maintains an extensive archive of his papers and work, including more than one thousand drawings and two thousand items of correspondence dealing with his career through 1968.